His innocence lost (uncle Earl)

By:Anthony Hawkins

ISBN:978-1-312-65929-2

Cover Art By Anthony Hawkins

Dedicated to the gay and lesbian community.

Warning:This book contains graphic explicit and mature content.

Prologue

It was a hot midnight in the month of july,and Latrelle was expecting company.Latrelle was single and lived alone,just her and her young 1 year old son Taye.Latrelle was light skin,had honey brown colored eyes,and a full figure,and her young son Taye resembled her in many of his features,having her honey brown colored eyes,and her full pink lips and light skin,skin that was smooth like butter.

Stop that fucking crying boy,Latrelle rocked Taye back and forth in her arms with annoyance.Young Taye cried and cried,even while being rocked,and this drove Latrelle nearly insane.Boy shut the fuck up,imma about to call your father to come get your ass,nigga dont never claim you! Latrelle screamed to Taye,Taye still crying,tears filling his tiny brown eyes.Latrelle placed Taye into his crib that stood next to her bed,and then sat down on her own bed as she allowed him to cry,turning up her radio to it's full volume.Taye's cries were overpowered by the loud hiphop music escaping from Latrelle's radio.Latrelle felt sort of guilty,and then decided to turn off her radio as she scooped Taye back into her arms again,placing a pacifier into his crying mouth.

There,you got your binky now,so cut that shit out,Latrelle spoke to Taye,Taye now quiet.Latrelle rocked Taye for a few more minutes and then placed him into his crib once he began to fall asleep.Someone was knocking at Latrelle's door,their fists beating hard against the front door of her house.Who the fuck is it?!

Latrelle yelled as she headed to the front door,closing her blouse just a bit.It's me,Souja,open up chick,a deep male voice spoke to Latrelle.Nigga you knocking hard like that when you know Taye be sleeping around this time? Latrelle spoke to Souja as she pulled her front door open,now staring at his six foot tall figure and dark skin.Yall young niggas be on some other stuff,yall like to get straight to the point dont yall,this pussy aint on sale today nigga,Latrelle spoke to Souja.

Souja was a few years younger than Latrelle,at least nearly 10 years younger,Souja was a 20 year old,while Latrelle was 29 going on 30.Many people looked down on Latrelle and Souja's relationship,saying that Souja was too young for her,tho Latrelle and Souja just ignored it.So can i get a kiss or something? Souja questioned Latrelle.Latrelle stood to her tiptoes and then gave Souja a kiss on the lips as he leaned down to kiss her back.

Them lips on fire tonight boo,Latrelle spoke to Souja,flirting with him a little.They the bestest girl,and you love them,Souja boasted to Latrelle,giving her behind a squeeze.Alright,keep it down,my little dude sleep,Latrelle explained to Souja silently as she took him to the sofa.Man that little nigga cry too much,my pops would've broke my damn neck if i cried like that,he going be a little punk,Souja spoke to Latrelle.Nigga dont be talking about my child like that,he just a mamas boy,he going be alright,Latrelle smiled at Souja.Whatever,give me some loving,Souja began to kiss Latrelle,his hands grabbing her waist.Soon Souja was on top of Latrelle,while her back laid to the sofa.Latrelle and Souja made love that night,while Taye slept the entire night away in the other room.

Latrelle jumped to her feet from the sofa the next morning,hearing Taye's loud cries in the next room.Latrelle quickly ran into her bedroom to check on Taye,taye on his knees in his crib crying,tears sliding down his innocent face.Latrelle was about to take Taye into her arms,but Souja stopped her.Man let him cry,let him get it outta his system,you spoil that little nigga,let's go in the other room,Souja explained to Latrelle.Souja wrapped his muscled and tattooed arms around Latrelle and then smooth talked her back into the other room,Latrelle ignoring Taye's cries,and souja shutting the door behind them,not wanting to hear Taye's screams.Would if he hurting somewhere Souja,imma go check on him,Latrelle spoke to Souja.Naw,let him cry,he going stop eventually,Souja kissed Latrelle,holding her in his arms as they sat on the sofa.

Latrelle was the type of woman that put a male lovers needs before the needs of her own flesh in blood,her child.

Chapter 1

3 years passed,and Taye was now a 4 year old,and could walk and talk,tho his speech still needed work due to his young age.Man stop leaving your fucking crayons on the floor man,Souja spoke to Taye.Sorry,mommy said i could color,Taye spoke to Souja in his small

child voice.Clean that shit up before your moms get home,she got me watching you and shit,like i aint got other shit to do,pick that shit up,Souja ordered Taye.Taye began to pick up his crayons,obeying Souja's orders.Nigga and next time dont get fucking smart,i aint ask you if your moms said you could color,i told you to stop leaving crayons on the fucking floor! Souja smacked Taye in the back of his head as taye picked up his crayons.Taye began to cry,feeling the sting of Souja's big hand against the back of his skull.

Shut that shit up nigga,stop being a little pussy! Souja yelled at Taye.Nigga imma give you something to cry for,Souja spoke as he took off his belt and then began to whip Taye with it,causing Taye to scream out even louder.Sit your ass on the couch! Souja swung Taye onto the sofa by his arm,Taye crying at the far edge,huge tears escaping his eyes.You better shut that shit up little nigga or you going get it again,Souja warned Taye.Taye forced his cries and tears in,sniffing just a little,trying to hold back his emotions.

Come over here,Souja spoke as he reached for Taye,sitting him in his lap.Crying like a little girl and shit,Souja spoke to Taye as he pulled down Taye's tiny underwear.Souja then scooted himself up a bit as he pulled something of his own down,sitting Taye back on his lap again.Cry and watch what i do nigga,Souja scolded Taye,placing his hands around Taye's tiny waist.Taye began crying as he lurched up and down on something painful.Souja pulled his hand around Taye's mouth,wanting to muffle Taye's

crying during their inappropriate
moment.

Give me that little pussy nigga,Souja
spoke to Taye as he bit down on his
lip,Taye seeming as if he was
bouncing on Souja's knee,tho he
quite wasn't.Souja began to moan as
he began breathing down Taye's tiny
neck,giving him kisses on the neck
area,but not innocent and
affectionate kisses.Souja bounced
Taye one last time,and then let out a
sigh of relief,pushing Taye off of his
lap afterwards.

Souja grabbed a cloth from the bathroom closet,and then cleaned himself off,and then going back over to Taye to do the same to him.Here,wipe your ass nigga,it's just something that happens to real men,it's just water i put on you,dont be telling your moms a damn thing,real men dont run their fucking mouth,Souja explained to Taye after handing him a cloth,Taye too young to understand anything that happened between him and Souja,just knowing it was something that happened to him once every now and then,only when Latrelle was away.

A few knocks came at the front door,the knock catching Souja's ears.Souja pulled Taye's clothes back up and then headed to the front door,answering it with an attitude.Who is it?! Souja questioned the visitor at the door angrily.It's Earl,a male voice spoke.Nigga dont you got your own place man? Souja spoke to the man Earl as he opened the door.Nigga whatever,im here to pick up Taye,where my nephew at? Earl spoke to Souja.

He in there,take that little nigga,boy spoiled,Souja spoke to Earl.Earl was a few feet shorter than Souja,and was petite and well mannered,his head bald.There go my little nephew,you ready to get your hair cut? Earl spoke to Taye as he headed toward him,Taye grinning back at him with glee.

Hi uncle Earl,Taye smiled.Come give your unc a hug boy,Earl demanded Taye.Taye jumped from the sofa and then walked over to Earl,his walking kind of strange and unusual to Earl.Boy why you walking like that,you alright? Earl spoke to Taye,his face serious.Leave the little nigga alone,he alright,Souja intervened quickly.Naw,something aint right,what your leg hurt? Earl spoke to Taye.No,Taye shook his head.What your ass hurt? Earl questioned Taye again.Yes,i mean no,Taye shook his head yes and then no,unsure of how to answer Earl's question,his eyes flickering back and forth to Souja and then Earl.

Boy what you hit your ass on something? Earl asked Taye as he scooped him up into his arms.You ready for your haircut? Earl spoke to Taye.Yes uncle Earl,Taye smiled widely at Earl as Earl took him out the door,Souja shutting the door behind them.

Chapter 2

Earl handed Taye a lollipop after getting Taye's hair cut.You looking good little man,your hair on point,Earl spoke to Taye,making Taye feel special.Thank you uncle Earl,Taye smiled.Earl grabbed Taye into his arms and then began to make plane sounds as he playfully swung him around like an airplane.Taye giggled as Earl playfully used him as an airplane.Ow! Taye shouted out.You alright? Earl questioned Taye as he placed him back to the ground.It hurts,Taye explained to Earl.

What hurts? Earl questioned Taye with concern.Down here,Taye pointed to his posterior.Come on,imma about to take you to the hospital,let me call your mother right quick,Earl spoke to Taye as he reached for his hand and then took him across the street to his car.

Earl pulled out his cellphone and then began to call Latrelle.Hello? Latrelle answered Earl's phone call.Yea this Earl,Taye said his little booty hurt,so imma about to take him to the hospital alright,Earl explained to Latrelle.His butt hurt? he probably was showing out,thats why,Latrelle spoke to Earl.Yea,i know how kids is,but imma take him to the hospital anyway,just to be sure,Earl explained to Latrelle.Well alright,you his uncle Earl,go ahead,but bring him back home around eight,he going go see his nana on his father side,Latrelle spoke to Earl.Alright,Earl ended he and Latrelle's call.

Earl took Taye to the hospital,where the doctors closely examined him.Earl sat in the waiting room,and then was soon approached by two police officers.My nephew ok,whats going on? Earl questioned the stern looking police officers.Your nephew is ok but we cant release him into your custody sir,one of the police officers explained to Earl.What you mean,thats my nephew,what the fuck going on? Earl spoke to the police officers,his anger beginning to rise.Calm down sir,we can easily arrest you for using profane publicly,the officer spoke to Earl.

Man this bullshit! Earl shouted.Get him outta here,the officer spoke to his partner,the other officer handcuffing Earl and then escorting him down the big hospital hallway.That aint right man,where is my nephew? Earl spoke to the police officer.He's ok,we told you before sir,but we have a few questions to ask you,the officer spoke to Earl as he took him into a secluded room,the other officer joining them.Have you ever touched your nephew? one of the officers questioned Earl.Hell no,thats my fam,im not his biological uncle but that boy is like my own blood,Earl explained to the officer.Have you ever fondled your nephew,we take cases like this very seriously sir,answer the question in truth,have you ever sexually abused your nephew? the officer questioned Earl again sternly.

No,like i said the first time,i would never do some nasty shit like that to a child,my nephew at that,Earl spoke in honesty to the officers.Ok,we're taking your word,but we done some research on you,you hangout at a gay bar from time to time am i right? one of the officers questioned Earl.Yea,im an openly gay male,and your point is? Earl caught attitude with the officers.Nothing,we're done here,the officers explained to each other and Earl.Naw,you trying say that because im gay i touched my nephew inappropriately,thats what yall saying,i aint stupid,thats some stereotypical foul shit man,Earl spoke to the officers,the officers wielding guilty facial expressions.

Before we let you go we need a dna sample from you,one officer spoke to Earl.Yall still aint tell me where all this bs coming from,huh? Earl spoke to the officers with anger.Sir your nephew was given a full examination,and male semen was found in his cavity sir,are there any other males who care for him,anyone we could check with? the officer spoke to Earl.Shit man,so you telling me my nephew been getting molested? Earl shook his head in disgust.Unfortunately the boys checkup is accurate sir,sir if you know anybody else we could check with please let us know,the officers explained to Earl as they took him down the hallway,and then to be eventually dna tested.

Chapter 3

Latrelle arrived at the hospital an hour later,worry in her eyes.Where my baby?! Latrelle questioned the police officers and doctors about Taye's whereabouts.He's ok maam,he's in the examining room,an officer spoke to Latrelle,escorting her to the room,a doctor assisting them.The doctors insisted young Taye stay over night,and he did.

Your free to go sir,your dna didn't match the sperm samples we found in your nephew,we're sorry for the confusion,an officer explained to Earl.Man yall had me in here like i was some kind of criminal,but yall need to find out who did touch my nephew,that should be yall next move,Earl spoke as he took his face out of his palms,his face strained and stressed.The boys mother,your nephews mother wants a few words with you,the officer spoke to Earl.The officer then headed into Taye's room,and then came back out with Latrelle and Taye.Latrelle slowly approached Earl with watery eyes,Taye resting in her arms.You no good Earl,you was like a brother to me,and you going pull some shit like this,huh? Latrelle spoke to Earl.Man i didn't do a damn thing to Taye,i love that boy,you know that shit Latrelle,Earl explained to Latrelle.

Uh,uh,i aint having that,i dont want you around my house,i dont want you picking Taye up no more either,you aint shit to me no more,i swear on that,Latrelle explained to Earl.You do know im not a match right,my dna didn't match what they found up inside boy,you talking a bunch of bullshit right now,you really can sit here and think i touched Taye inappropriately? Earl spoke to Latrelle.I dont know what to think right now Earl,and then i find out you gay,when was i going find this out,how many more secrets you got? Latrelle spoke to Earl.What the fuck that got to do with anything Latrelle,i didn't touch Taye,im fucking sticking by that,it's sad that a gay man cant love a boy child without being considered a fucking pedo,i cant take this shit,Earl chuckled,hiding his anger behind it.

He a little boy Earl,how can you put your thing in a little boy? Latrelle spoke to Earl,tears streaming down her face.Man fuck you Latrelle,tell Taye i love him,im gone man,i would give him a kiss on his forehead before i go,but then imma have yall motherfuckers making accusations,and you let Taye know he gotta place to stay whenever he need it in the future,im not going let you or nobody else stop me from having a relationship with that boy,i been there since day one,day one Latrelle,bye man,Earl stormed out of the hospital,his fist balled.

Uncle Earl,why is uncle Earl leaving us? Taye questioned Latrelle as he woke just in time to see Earl leave out the hospital,this was the last time Taye or Latrelle saw Earl.Mommy is Souja going to leave too,the big men with the guns asked me if uncle Earl touched my butt,why did they ask me that,is uncle Earl in trouble,uncle Earl's nice,i didn't tell on anybody,especially not Souja,Souja told me that real men dont run their mouths,is Souja going to be in trouble mommy? Taye ranted silently.

Latrelle quickly carried Taye into a quiet and secluded corner of the hospital away from the doctors and police officers,and then began speaking to him in a low voice.Sh,baby keep quiet,you going get Souja in trouble,you need a man in your life,Souja just looking out for you,i aint having you grow up gay,you remember i told you it's wrong in the eyes of the lord,being around your uncle Earl too much can start messing with you,and i dont wanna hear you say nothing about Souja around them police officers or them doctors,you hear me,dont even tell them Souja living with us if they ask you,Latrelle explained to Taye very silently,not wanting to get Souja into trouble,even tho the things Taye said to her were somewhat suspicious,her false love for Souja clouding her judgement.

Latrelle sent the police on a wild goose chase,telling them that she once saw a man eyeing Taye at a local playground,tho she was lying.The investigation of Taye's sexual abuse simmered down after awhile,and Latrelle made sure to keep a low profile,keeping the police and medical examiners away from her door.

Chapter 4

One afternoon Latrelle and Souja and now 5 year old Taye all went out to the grocery store,tho Souja insisted he wait in the car,letting Latrelle do the shopping,Latrelle leaving Taye with him.The car was quiet,Taye and

Souja both sitting silently, Taye in the backseat, and Souja in the front seat, the steering wheel just above his knees.

Ay Taye get up in the front seat man, Souja ordered Taye smoothly, his eyes staring out the car window. Taye climbed into the passenger seat, and then sat silently beside Souja, his tiny hands in his lap. Souja then turned to meet Taye with a blank expression, and then eased Taye's tiny hands below his belt, Taye looking helpless. The buckle of Souja's belt rattled as he unfastened it, letting something fall from his slightly unzipped denim pants.You feel that little dude,look how hard you got it,you see it? Souja whispered to Taye,Taye's face confused.Is mommy going to take really long in the store? Taye questioned Souja.Your moms alright,you just do what you gotta do nigga,Souja explained to Taye sternly.

Souja moved Taye's hand up and down his pole looking equipment,and then allowed Taye to handle the taboo piece of equipment himself.Is that milk stuff going to come out again? Taye questioned Souja innocently.Nigga shut up,and just keep doing it,Souja spoke to Taye,his moans getting louder.Nigga hurry up,your moms coming out the store! Souja warned Taye,seeing Latrelle exit the grocery store,tho she had a ways to get back to the car,the car being parked all the way at the corner of the grocery store.

Fuck yea little nigga,choke that shit,hurry up,Souja moaned,and then soon something spilling into Taye's hand followed by Souja's loud and deep grunt.Fuck,shit,you beat that nut out little nigga,get back in the back seat,hurry up man,Souja commanded Taye,helping Taye climb back to the back seat by his rear,and then quickly fastening his belt and pants again.

There go my little man,both of my two favorite men,Latrelle spoke to Taye and Souja as she got to the car,placing grocery bags in the trunk,and then handing Taye a pack of gummy bears.

Boy what is this shit on your hands,you always getting into

something,what you then got into? Latrelle spoke to Taye angrily,seeing a thick wet substance on his hand as she handed him the pack of gummy bears.He was back there playing in lotion and shit,Souja quickly explained to Latrelle,realizing that he had forgotten to clean up the evidence of he and Taye's inappropriate encounter.Taye i should beat your ass boy,Souja hand me them wipes up there in the storage,Latrelle spoke,using the wipes Souja handed her to clean Taye's hand of the assumed lotion she thought it was.

Latrelle sat up at the passenger side seat next to Souja after cleaning up Taye,giving Souja a quick kiss on the lips before she pulled a seat belt around her shoulder.Souja then placed his hands on the steering wheel of the car,pulling out of the parking lot of the grocery store,and then hitting the highway,Taye sitting in the back,his pack of gummy bears resting in his tiny hands.

The indecent cycle between Taye and Souja continued for years to come.

Chapter 5

14 years passed,and Taye was now a handsome 18 year old young man with smooth clear skin and a very slender but toned body,with a backside that was firm and round,and abs that were very noticeable,and hair that was jet black,cut short and wavy.Taye get your ass out here! Latrelle called out to Taye.Huh ma? Taye spoke to Latrelle while straining his eyes to see,him being waken up by Latrelle's voice,his own voice

mature now,tho he still had somewhat boyish looks.

What the fuck is this,you better tell me something? Latrelle spoke to Taye as she flashed a cellphone in front of his eyes.Ma you was going through my phone? Taye spoke as he reached for the phone in Latrelle's hand.You damn right,this my house,Latrelle snatched the cellphone away from Taye before he could latch his fingers around it.Boy what is this,this better be a female talking to you like this,but the person name is Brandon,thats the problem i got,talking about baby i get at you later,who is this texting you Taye? Latrelle spoke to Taye as her eyes continued to scan through the text messages on Taye's cellphone screen.Ma thats a homey of mine,can i have my phone back? Taye spoke to Latrelle with annoyance.

Uh,uh,a homey,homeys dont talk to each other like this,then this other message say oh meet me tomorrow,i want them cakes,explain this shit to me Taye,you better give me a good answer,im waiting? Latrelle spoke to Taye,guilt all over his face.He just a friend ma,Taye said stiffly to Latrelle.Lie to me again,who is this dude calling you baby,and sending you all these nasty ass texts talking about he wanna fuck again,who Taye? Latrelle spoke to Taye sternly.Just keep my phone ma,im not about to do this today,i wish i wouldn't have left my phone on the table man,Taye turned around to go into his bedroom,wanting to avoid answering Latrelle's question.Boy turn back around,im not picking on you,i just dont wanna see you live that kind of lifestyle,being gay aint a

path i want for you,Latrelle explained
to Taye.

I cant tell you who to be friends
with,but i just want you to be
careful,remember that everything
you do in the dark will come to the
light,Latrelle spoke to Taye,giving him
his cellphone back and then heading
in the other direction.Taye placed his
phone into the pocket of his sweat
pants and then went back into his
bedroom,sitting on his bed,placing
his face into his palms.Taye felt
exposed,Latrelle discovering his

sexual orientation through cellphone texts he made with another male.

Taye stood to his feet again,and then searched for Latrelle,finding her in her bedroom alone on her bed watching the television set.Ma,can i come in? Taye questioned Latrelle.Just come on in,Latrelle answered Taye.Taye then got onto her bed,snuggling beside her,and then began to speak.

Im sorry for turning my back on you ma,Taye spoke to Latrelle.It's ok baby,i shouldn't have overreacted the way i did,Latrelle then spoke.Now leave me alone,my show on,Latrelle spoke to Taye.Taye then headed out of her room and then back into his own,checking his texts.

The hours flew pass,and soon Taye could hear someone knocking on his bedroom door.Who is it? Taye answered his bedroom door,cracking his door open slightly.Just open your door man,Souja spoke to Taye,forcing himself in as Taye stumbled to the side.Your moms told me about some nigga you got sending you gay ass messages,whats up with that? Souja spoke to Taye.Man it's just a friend of mine,Taye explained to Souja.Naw,that aint no friend,me and my boys dont talk to each other like that,let me see your phone,Souja spoke to Taye,Taye's face covered with guilt.Taye got his cellphone from off of his dresser and then handed it to Souja.Nigga open up the texts,i dont know where you keep your shit saved,Souja explained to Taye,seeing just a blank screen on Taye's cellphone,no texts.

Taye then took his phone back from Souja,opening up his saved texts,and then handing it back to him.Souja's eyes scanned the text messages from Taye's male friend.Nigga this dont seem like a friend my man,this seem like some gay shit,shit aint cool,Souja spoke to Taye.You know that shit aint going down in this house right,not up in this piece,Souja explained to Taye.I said dude just a friend man,Taye lied to Souja.I heard you the first time,but these motherfucking texts say differently little dude,and who is you raising your voice at? Souja shoved Taye with one of his hands.Man im

18,can i at least be friends with who i wanna be friends with,i mean it's not like im bringing them over,can i at least have that? Taye explained calmly to Souja.

Wont you at least have this nigga,have that,Souja shoved Taye again,Taye stumbling backwards,but then catching himself before he could fall.Souja i told you to just speak with him about the texts,but you need to calm down right now,come on in the room,Latrelle spoke to Souja,seeing that Souja was beginning to lose his temper with Taye.Naw,you told me to speak with him,and thats what im going do,bounce man! Souja forced Latrelle back out of Taye's bedroom,and then slamming the door shut,placing one of his hands over it,applying pressure to it,in order to keep Latrelle out.Latrelle banged on Taye's door but couldn't budge it,Souja still applying pressure to the door.

Alright,get over here,get on your knees,Souja ordered Taye.Naw man,Taye spoke to Souja.Nigga imma ask you one more time,get over here and get on your knees or imma crack your whole motherfucking dome,Souja spoke calmly to Taye.Taye eased himself towards Souja and then kneeled to his knees as Souja began pulling down his pants and underwear in front of Taye's eyes,Latrelle still banging hard against the door,trying to enter.Latrelle he going know how it is to be a mans bitch,Souja spoke to Latrelle from inside the room.Souja then placed his hand around Taye's head,forcing Taye's mouth onto his penis,tho Taye kept his mouth closed,Souja's penis grazing along his lips instead of inside his mouth.Open your fucking mouth nigga! Souja yelled at Taye,Taye's eyes becoming watery.Taye's fists began to ball,and his light colored face was flushed with anger.

You can ball up your fists if you want,you aint about nothing,open your fucking mouth nigga,Souja commanded Taye again,squeezing Taye's jaws.Taye finally gave in,and then slightly opened his mouth,Souja's penis penetrating it.Souja then removed Taye's mouth from his penis,and then shoved his penis back into Taye's mouth again,repeating the process.Taye's head bobbed back and forth on Souja's erect penis,until Souja began to grunt out loud.Taye figured what would happen next,so he quickly removed his mouth from Souja's penis,but Souja shoved himself back into Taye's mouth,grunting in pleasure as he ejaculated into Taye's mouth,Taye then backing away from Souja,spitting Souja's semen into his trashcan from his semen filled mouth.

Lesson learned little nigga,you can fuck with me if you want,you then got yourself a mouth full of nut,im out,Souja spoke to Taye as Taye gagged over the trashcan.Souja then swung the bedroom door open,nearly knocking Latrelle over as he left out,Latrelle beating him all over his chest and arms with her fists,furious of what he did to Taye,tho she didn't quite see it with her own eyes.Thats going make him stop liking dudes,what the fuck you fighting me for Latrelle,go ahead with that bullshit,why are you hitting me tho man?! Souja yelled at Latrelle,Taye still on his knees leaning over his trashcan in disgust.

Nigga you really asking me why im fucking you up when you just made my son suck your dick?! Latrelle continued to beat on Souja in heated anger,tho her blows didn't do much damage to him,Souja just blocking his face from time to time,but allowing Latrelle's other blows to make impact.Chill Latrelle,chill the fuck out man! Souja yelled,Latrelle still hitting on him.Alright,enough is enough man,cut that shit out! Souja shouted at Latrelle as he grabbed her by both her arms,just as she was about to hit him again.

Enough aint a motherfucking enough,imma fuck you up in here,you going do that shit to my son in my house,thats some triflin shit! Latrelle went berserk on Souja again,tears beginning to slide down her partly deranged facial expression.I love you Latrelle,i was helping your little dude,calm the fuck down man,give me a kiss,Souja sweet talked Latrelle,trying to calm her anger.You gotta get the fuck out,Latrelle spoke silently to Souja,her anger beginning to fade as Souja kissed her all over her neck,trying to soothe her.Souja get the fuck off me,im too fucking pissed at you right now,Latrelle spoke,then allowing Souja to ease her into her bedroom,shutting the door behind them.

Latrelle and Souja stayed in the bedroom for fifteen minutes,until Latrelle exited the room again,but not assisted by Souja.Taye sat on his bed silently,his thoughts wandering.Can i come in baby? Latrelle spoke softly to Taye as she stood at his doorway.You can come in ma,Taye said silently,his eyes staring at the floor.Baby im so fucking sorry for what Souja did to you,that man can get carried away sometimes,but he mean well,now he took it too far by putting his thing in your face like that,but he love you,just try and get along with him baby,you know how he is,you been around him since you was little,he do love you,i know he do,Latrelle explained to Taye,a part of her believing what she said and a part of her not believing it.

Taye eyed Latrelle silently,feeling that she was being delusional,tho he didn't question her judgement.Ma imma see if i can stay with one of my friends for awhile,just until i find my own place,Taye explained to Latrelle calmly,his face emotionless.Baby you dont got to leave,work things out here first,dont just up and leave,and you dont wanna stay with just anybody,some of them type of people you be around aint nothing but bad news,Latrelle spoke to Taye.What people are you talking about ma,who,people like Brandon,and me? Taye admitted to his same sex sexual orientation to Latrelle.Baby just sleep on it,stay here where you got people you know,now imma go back in the room and finish talking to Souja,while i

want you to think about what i said
to you,Latrelle spoke to Taye,and
then silently leaving out of his
bedroom,closing his door shut behind
her.

Taye sat up nearly all night thinking
about what Souja had did to him,and
tho he wanted to leave,he felt that he
would be a burden on whom ever he
chose to live with,and thought that
maybe he could work things out at
home,just maybe.Latrelle thought
that if Taye left that he would
become even more involved with the
gay culture,and wanted to keep him

to herself.Tho Latrelle was furious about what Souja had done to Taye she still had an excessive and unhealthy need for Souja,no matter how vile he was to Taye and even her.

Chapter 6

A week had passed,and Taye was just heading in the house from a night out with one of his friends.Taye headed into his bedroom and then tossed his overshirt on his bed,kicking his shoes off afterwards,and then sitting on his bed.Taye's cellphone began to ring,Taye easing it out of his pants pocket to answer it.Whats up Brandon? Taye answered his phone,Seeing Brandon's name on his caller id.Shit man,i was wondering if you wanted to hang out a little later,i'll come scoop you up,you down? Brandon spoke to Taye.I would come out with you,but i just got in the house man,im just chilling right now,we can chill tomorrow tho man,Taye explained to Brandon.

I got you,so what you doing for the rest of the night man? Brandon questioned Taye.Nothing,probably see whats on tv,Taye spoke to Brandon.Your moms boyfriend still giving you shit? Brandon spoke to Taye.He been alright,he haven't been really fucking with me lately,dude kinda chill right now,Taye explained to Brandon.That nigga is crazy or something,was he like that when you was little? Brandon spoke to Taye.Honestly man i dont even remember,i can only remember bits and pieces,like i remember this one time that dude beat my ass for some dumb shit,i was like 7 or something,Taye explained to

Brandon,only remembering a few things Souja did to him,not quite remembering the sexual abuse,him being extremely young at the time.

The sexual abuse from Souja stopped once Taye reached a certain age,Souja fearing that Taye wouldn't be easy to control and manipulate as he once was,and that Taye might have began to speak about their many inappropriate moments,Souja knowing he would be in trouble due to his sex acts with a minor.

Man if my moms had a boyfriend like yours do i would be in jail for killing that nigga,Brandon explained to Taye,chuckling afterwards.Taye joined in on Brandon's laughter,and then suddenly paused,seeing Souja walking silently to his open bedroom door.

Ay Brandon imma call you back,Taye said quietly and quickly to Brandon as Souja got closer.Man you alright,why you talking all low and trying get me off the phone and shit? Brandon laughed,his laughs echoing through the phone.Naw,dont tell that nigga to hang up,i can hear that nigga all the way from here,nigga cackling like a motherfucking schoolgirl,Souja spoke to Taye.Thats that nigga that was sending you them gay ass texts aint it? Souja questioned Taye.Imma call you back man,hang up,Taye spoke to Brandon again,fear in his eyes.Give me your motherfucking phone,give me that shit,imma about to end this shit right now,Souja snatched Taye's cellphone from out of his hand.Hello,who the fuck is this? Souja questioned Brandon,Brandon hesitating to answer at first.This

Brandon,who this? Brandon spoke to Souja smoothly.

Aint none of your motherfucking business who this is,dont call this motherfucking phone again,delete the number out your phone or unsave the shit i dont care,but if you call this phone again you going get Taye fucked up,and imma fuck your little ass up too if i ever catch you on the street little nigga! Souja explained to Brandon.Naw man,i wasn't trying to be disrespectful,Brandon spoke calmly to Souja,slight fear in his voice.Yea whatever nigga,Souja hung up the phone in Brandon's ear before he could speak another word.You still with them same games Taye,you still with that faggot shit,just tell me man,you still got dudes calling your phone like you their bitch or something? Souja spoke to Taye,slight anger on his face.

Man my business is my business,just let me be dawg,i try my best to stay on your good side,but you stay giving me shit! Taye spoke out to Souja,his face angered.Nigga who is you talking to like that,man i would fuck you up in this bitch,try me little nigga,do something,Souja pushed himself against Taye,Taye not backing down,tho he was scared of Souja,Souja placing fear in him since childhood,the kind of fear that didn't just disappear overnight.

Man im not about to go there with you Souja,you was the only dude in the house when i was growing up,i respect you,but im not going have you rolling up on me anytime you feel like it man,Taye explained to Souja,Souja chuckling in response,a sinister chuckle.Nigga you really trying my patiences right now,you really thinking you tough right now nigga,like i wont snatch your little ass up,grown or not,i will give your ass a good ass whooping just like i used to do when you was little,try your hand nigga! Souja spoke to Taye as he still stood tall above Taye,his muscled chest poking against Taye's,their foreheads nearly meeting.

I cant believe your little pretty boy ass trying mouth off at me and shit,soft ass nigga,how your little pretty mouth like the taste of my dick,you just ate them nuts up didn't you,you liked it you punk ass nigga?

Souja spoke to Taye,hoping to provoke him by bringing up their previous forced sexual encounter.You wrong man,get the fuck away from me man,Taye shoved Souja away from him.Thats what i was waiting for nigga,get tough,and imma about to tear your little ass up! Souja yanked Taye by his shirt collar,Taye fidgeting to break away from his strong grip.

Get the fuck off of me Souja! Taye yelled.Bring your ass here nigga,Souja roughed Taye up,eventually turning Taye over on his stomach,Taye shouting in anger.You think you tough nigga,huh,think i cant check your ass no more,is that what it is?! Souja spoke to Taye,forcing Taye's underwear down as Taye struggled.

There we go,that ass in the open now,Souja began to violently spank Taye on his exposed posterior,wanting to whip Taye into submission,hoping he would keep Taye obedient to him.Souja then tossed Taye into the hallway from his bedroom,Taye squirming on the cool hardwood floor,his pants and underwear at his knees.

Souja what the fuck is you doing?! Latrelle screamed at Souja as she entered the area,seeing Taye crawling to his knees.Mind your business Latrelle,imma teach this little nigga! Souja yelled at Latrelle as she approached.Look at this nigga crawling,where you going nigga? Souja grabbed Taye up as Taye began to crawl to his feet,trying to escape.In the room nigga,in the motherfucking room! Souja carried Taye back into his bedroom by the back of his neck.

I cant take this! Latrelle screamed out in tears,shutting herself into her bedroom,not wanting to see the violent situation between Taye and Souja,but not intervening either.Souja took Taye into his bedroom,and then slammed the door shut,locking it,Taye's screams being heard through the closed door.Latrelle balled herself up into a corner and then turned on her radio,turning the volume up,not wanting to hear Taye's screams,the pain in Taye's screams filling her with agony,and slight guilt.

Little red ass nigga,you want something up in that sweet gay ass dont you? Souja fondled with Taye's rear,groping it.You grown huh,you a man now Taye,huh?! Souja continued to manhandle Taye,and then squeezing Taye's posterior again,harassing Taye with violent and sexual threats nearly through the entire night,then eventually leaving Taye alone in his bedroom,Taye shaken up,disturbed and silently nestled on his bed,tears running down his face.

Souja's abuse continued day after day,Souja trying to find any reason he could to harass Taye,no matter how petty the reason.Souja openly became more sexually abusive to Taye,seeing that Latrelle tolerated it,and no longer said anything about it,just to please him.

Chapter 7

Souja sat at the kitchen table with his legs gapped,a cup of liqour resting in his hands,Latrelle sitting not too far from him on the other side,her face stressed and drained.Taye entered the house silently from a day at the new school he attended,his eyes making contact with Souja and Latrelle.Hey ma,hey Souja,Taye spoke silently to Latrelle and Souja as he closed the front door behind him,placing the locks on.

Nigga dont keep the door open like that next time,people are motherfucking nosy,Souja spoke to Taye.Hey baby,how was school,you like the teachers,how is the students,i know these young kids today,they aint wild like how they was in highschool are they? Latrelle spoke to Taye.Yea,let's hope he aint meet no nigga up in there,i know a few niggas probably would love to jump on his little red ass,Souja added sarcastically to Latrelle's words.

The school big,and the teachers kinda laid back,the students cool too,Taye explained to Latrelle as he bent to pick up his backpack again,swinging it over his shoulder.Latrelle gave Souja a dirty look as she saw his eyes roam towards Taye's posterior,just as Taye bent to get his bag.Alright baby,you go ahead in do your homework or whatever,imma just sit my ass in this chair,im tired,Latrelle spoke to Taye,hoping to get Taye out of the kitchen.Alright,Taye spoke to Latrelle,and then headed into his bedroom,shutting his door behind him.

Souja im not trying nag you,but did you ever fuck dudes while you was in prison,you went to prison when you was 18,and you was in there until you was like 20,that was around the time i met you,but like said,keep it real,did you ever fuck any dudes in there,i know your stuff had to get hard every

now and then,so did you? Latrelle
spoke to Souja,Souja's facial
expression turning unpleasant.

What you mean did i ever fuck any
dudes in prison? Souja frowned at
Latrelle.Im just saying,i didn't say you
did,im just asking you if you did,stop
being jumpy,and then when you
pulled your thing out i front of Taye
my mind really got to wondering,i
know you was trying help him,but me
and my homegirl was talking,and she
said a nigga dick cant just get hard for
another man,it gotta be something
about the other man that turned him

on to begin with,because i thought you like doing that to Taye for a hot minute,Latrelle explained to Souja,Souja staring at her angrily.

Your homegirl need to mind her fucking business,and you keep listening to her and maybe i bounce out this bitch,Souja stormed from the table,leaving Latrelle alone in the kitchen.Baby i didn't mean to make you mad! Latrelle spoke out to Souja,apologizing,Souja slamming their bedroom door behind him,ignoring her.Souja was a highly conflicted person,having issues with his anger,his sexuality,and many more things as well.

Chapter 8

Taye grew closer to one of his teachers at school,a man who the students called professor E.Professor E was a very kind and gentle man,but kept to himself,keeping his relationship with his students strictly student and teacher,only chatting with them during school hours,but that changed after he met with Taye,Professor E revealing to Taye that they had a somewhat history afterschool,after grading one of Taye's exams,seeing Taye's full name.

Yea man,im your uncle Earl,you was my little nephew,well my big nephew now,you then grew up on me,but how is your mama doing? Professor E spoke to Taye,revealing himself to be Earl,Taye's caring uncle from years ago,the uncle that got falsely accused of Taye's molestation.Man i didn't even know i had family around these parts,i guess you learn something new everyday,Taye spoke to Earl with a warm smile,Earl smiling back widely,still excited to see Taye.We gotta lot of catching up to do youngster,boy i used to take you mostly everywhere i went,to the barber,the playground,shid,you name it man,i been missing you man,damn i been missing you,you just dont know,Earl spoke to Taye,pulling his arm around Taye's shoulder.Your mother still messing with that good for nothing nigga Souja? Earl questioned Taye,waiting for Taye to answer.Yea,she is,Taye spoke to Earl silently.

Ask your mother if i can stop pass the house a little later,this aint enough time for us to reconnect man,Earl spoke to Taye.Alright,imma do that,but if you dont hear from me i catch you next monday man,i mean uncle Earl,Taye jokingly smirked at Earl,Earl playfully shoving him away afterwards.Get your ass home,dont be out all night long boy! Earl waved at Taye as Taye headed off to his car,starting it and then pulling off,fleeing the school and Earl.

Taye headed home and then eased himself into the house,not seeing anyone in sight,the house dark and silent.Taye headed into his bedroom and then sat down on his bed,checking his text messages.

You know the drill nigga,let me see that phone man,Souja ordered Taye,his hands ready to recieve Taye's cellphone,so that he could search for any texts Taye may have recieved from Brandon or any other male he suspected Taye of having same sex relationships with.Taye handed his cellphone to Souja,and then watched as Souja's eyes scanned through his text messages.Souja tossed Taye's cellphone on the bed after he was done checking it,and then silently walked out of Taye's room.

Souja headed into the kitchen for a glass of orange juice as Taye headed to Latrelle's bedroom.

Ma,Taye tapped on Latrelle's bedroom door.Here i come baby,huh? Latrelle spoke to Taye as she opened her bedroom door.Ma this teacher at my school said he know me,he know you and Souja too,Taye explained to Latrelle.Who you talking about Taye,what teacher? Latrelle questioned Taye,her face confused.Yea,this dude,his name Earl,dude seem cool,he said he my uncle,i didn't even know you had a brother ma? Taye smiled at Latrelle,Latrelle's face kind of shocked.Baby come in here for a minute,i gotta have a talk with you right quick,Latrelle spoke to Taye,pulling him into her bedroom,and then closing the door.You cool ma,whats wrong? Taye questioned Latrelle.What he tell you baby,you didn't tell him where we

live now did you? Latrelle spoke to
Taye.

He aint tell me nothing,just that he
knew me from way back and shit like
that,and naw i didn't tell him where
we lived,he didn't even ask,Taye
explained to Latrelle.

Dont be telling Earl where we
live,and i dont even want you
associating with him too much,Earl
aint your real uncle,you used to call
him uncle Earl,but he aint your
uncle,me and him had a falling out

about you awhile back,Latrelle explained to Taye.Why,what happened? Taye spoke to Latrelle.He just wasn't the right kind of man i wanted around you growing up,Earl gay baby,and i wasn't having it,next thing you know you would've been gay too if i kept him around,now i know you got them dudes texting you,but you just going through a phase baby,i know you aint gay,Latrelle explained to Taye.Hold up,is Earl that dude that used to give me lollipops all the time after i got my hair cut? Taye questioned Latrelle.Yea,thats him,did he ever touch you baby,i know i asked you this when you was little,but did he? Latrelle spoke to Taye.

Naw,dude used to be fun to be around,what happened,why yall stop being cool,and why you ask me that ma? Taye spoke to Latrelle with confusion on his face.Baby i should have been told you,but you was touched when you was younger,you probably dont remember tho,you was young,Latrelle explained to Taye,Taye's facial expression becoming blank.Ma why you aint tell me none of this,how old was i? Taye spoke to Latrelle,his face annoyed.You was around 4,im sorry baby,Latrelle explained to Taye with tears in her eyes.Taye thought to himself long and hard,his memories scattered,but then rushing back to him with the sadness and horror it came with,the memories of Souja's verbal,physical,and sexual abuse all hitting him like a hammer to a nail.

Ma it wasn't no fucking Earl,it was Souja's bitch ass,Taye spoke angrily to Latrelle in tears,the memories of his sexual abuse now out in the open.Baby you sure,dont just be saying that baby,are you sure? Latrelle cried out to Taye as she pulled her arms around him tightly.Naw ma,get off me man,you just as bad as him,i cant take this no more,all these years of putting up with Souja is over man,im out,and i remember me telling you that that dude told me to not tell you nothing,and you took me in the corner and told me not to say shit,you probably knew and just didn't want to say shit to that nigga,Taye explained to Latrelle in deep emotion,removing her arms from around him.

Ma im about to take a shower and then pack my shit,and this might be the last time you see me,Taye explained stiffly to Latrelle,huge tears sliding down both their faces.

Taye gave Latrelle one last painful and tearful stare and then headed out of her bedroom and then into the bathroom,wanting to shower and then pack his things to go.Taye threw off all of his clothes from his body with anger,letting them hit the floor with a slight thump as he entered the bathroom.Taye then twisted the showerhead on,stepping his naked body into the bathtub,letting the steamy hot water run down his body.

Taye's thoughts began to circulate throughout his mind as he stood under the showerhead,he remembered the time his once tiny hands groped Souja's man part,and the outcome of it.Taye began soaping himself up,lathering the soap all over his body as his mind continued to wander.

Baby can i come in? Latrelle knocked on the bathroom door.Taye ignored

Latrelle,not wanting to speak to anyone at this point.Baby just let me speak to you ok,Latrelle spoke to Taye again outside of the bathroom door,sadness in her voice.What that nigga mad about? Souja asked Latrelle as he spotted her near the bathroom door,seeing that Taye was ignoring her.Dont talk to me right now Souja,i will hurt somebody right now,Latrelle spoke to Souja,anger in her face.What? Souja spoke to Latrelle.

You heard me,all this time it was you messing with Taye,thats why he used to always tell me his butt hurt,you a nasty ass motherfucker,and im partly at fault,a part of me knew something was going on between you and Taye,but i was so down and there for you that my stupid ass couldn't see straight,how could you fuck my baby Souja,he wasn't nothing but a baby,i trusted you around Taye,i thought you would be there for him like he was your own Souja,i should've been took your dick off when you tried that shit awhile ago with Taye,why you do that to my baby Souja,huh?! Latrelle yelled at Souja,and then began shoving him violently.Baby i love Taye,but that boy needed some stability man,i was helping him,Souja spoke softly to Latrelle as she continued to shove him back and forth,tears forming in her eyes.

Latrelle calm down man,you wilding right now! Souja spoke to Latrelle,grabbing both her hands,stopping her.Get the fuck off me! Latrelle yelled at Souja,yanking one of her hands away from him,and then smacking him across the face,the sound of her hands making impact with Souja's face echoing throughout the room.Man chill girl!

Souja began to manhandle Latrelle,causing her to scream out.Latrelle's screams caught Taye's ears as he quickly rinsed himself off and then stepped out of the tub naked and soaking wet.

Fuck this,Taye you wanna run your mouth like a pussy huh,huh you little half breed white looking punk,huh nigga?! Souja barged into the bathroom with Taye as he roughly pushed Latrelle aside to the floor,anger covering his face.Taye's heart nearly stopped as he examined Souja standing at the bathroom door in fear.You telling your moms i fucked you when you was little nigga,didn't i tell you about running your mouth like a bitch,what the fuck you tell your moms man?! Souja spoke to taye,Taye nervously staring back at him.

I just told her the truth man,you did used to mess with me when i was a boy man,i remember,i remember you sitting me in your lap dawg! Taye let the truth slip from his lips,feeling good in doing so,as if something was being lifted from his shoulder.Alright nigga,it's like that,huh,it's like that

Taye,i just fucked you all the time,so i never showed you no love,huh?! Souja yelled at Taye.You never showed me love man,the only time you was nice to me is when you wanted to get off sometimes,and not even all the time! Taye yelled back at Souja in deep anger.Nigga i was trying teach you how to be a man nigga,life is rough! Souja explained to Taye,admitting that he sexually abused Taye,but making any reason he could to justify himself sexually abusing Taye throughout the years,tho he himself knew that he was lying to not only Taye but himself also.

Souja calm down,Taye dont argue back with him baby,just hurry up and go in your room! Latrelle pleaded to Souja and Taye,seeing that their arguement was getting more serious by the second,and not wanting it to get out of hand.Naw,let the little nigga say what he gotta say! Souja spoke to Latrelle.Can i get pass man? Taye spoke to Souja as he pulled an above knee length white towel around the waist of his naked body,his eyes on Souja's face.I'll let you pass,but make me first nigga,Souja spoke to Taye,Taye exhaling in annoyance,knowing that Souja wanted to keep the trouble going.

Can i get pass dude,seriously,you did what you did to me man,im not even going snitch or nothing,i just wanna get out this house tonight dawg,can i get pass now? Taye spoke to Souja,easing his feet into flip flops at the same time.Who you talking to huh,huh Taye? Souja placed his forehead against Taye's,and then gripping his fingers around Taye's neck.

Souja then grazed his lips along Taye's cheek,the tip of his nose touching Taye's.Nigga i can do you just like i used to,and it's easy access this time,i aint gotta pull down them drawers this time,you hear me man? Souja spoke to Taye,threatening him.Do what you gotta do man,you aint going break me man,not no more,Taye spoke confidently to Souja.Here,since you gotta smart mouth nigga,suck on them fingers nigga,Souja forced his fingers into

Taye's mouth,pushing them back and forth,and then reaching his other hand down into his pants and underwear to masturbate himself.You like that little nigga,that remind you of that dick being in your mouth? Souja whispered to Taye as Taye ignored him.

Go ahead man,Taye shoved Souja's two fingers out of his mouth.Oh you fighting nigga,huh? Souja spoke to Taye,Taye becoming silent.Souja let him through,i swear on my life you aint doing my baby like that again,Latrelle grabbed Souja by his arms,Souja angrily pulling away from her.

Taye snuck pass Souja,Latrelle's intervention giving him time to get by Souja and out of the bathroom.Naw nigga,get the fuck back over here,where the fuck you going? Souja headed after Taye,nearly grabbing him by his arm,but then being startled by taps at the front door,Taye and Latrelle also being startled by the sounds.Auntie Latrelle,you there,im ready to get my hair braided,are you sleeping? a young girls voice spoke outside of the front door.Souja cool down,this little girl live down the street,i told her mother i would do her hair,Latrelle explained to Souja as she opened the front door.

Hey baby,you ready to get your hair done? Latrelle spoke to the little girl standing outside of her door,Latrelle quickly changing her mood from bad to good,faking it for the young girl at the door.Yes auntie Latrelle,the little girl spoke to Latrelle as Latrelle guided her inside,closing and locking the front door behind.

Go sit on the couch baby,i be over there,Latrelle explained to the little girl.Yes maam,the young girl spoke,obeying Latrelle's words,silently sitting on the couch as Latrelle headed over to her.Latrelle aint your aunt,she just know your moms,talking about auntie Latrelle,Souja spoke to the little girl,tho the little girl didn't quite hear him.Latrelle gave Souja a stare,wanting him to behave in front of their young guest,which was the little girl.

Hi Taye,the little girl waved at Taye with a big smile.Hi Kiana,Taye spoke back to the little girl silently,and then turning for his bedroom.Hi sir,Kiana waved at Souja as well,Souja ignoring her,and then setting his sight back on Taye.This aint over little nigga,you going get it,trust and believe man,Souja explained to Taye,and then headed into the bathroom to shower,slamming the door behind him,the little girl Kiana jumping slightly in fear in response of the slamming door.Kiana had unknowingly interrupted a bad situation that was only going to get worser had she not arrived at the door.

Souja peeled himself out of his clothes,and then pulled a stripy navy blue and baby blue towel around his waist as he headed back out to he and Latrelle's shared bedroom for a durag,not wanting his hair to get wet,his feet covered with clog slippers.You're strong sir,Kiana complimented Souja,and then blushing a bit afterwards,seeing Souja's tight abs and pecks and muscles flex as he walked back out from the bedroom.Souja was the type of man few people would believe to be a sexual abuser of young boys or children,and was very handsome when he wasn't being cruel,his silky and very dark skin highlighting his white straight teeth,and his handsome face smooth and shaven.

You strong,Souja mocked Kiana rudely.Man fuck this,i aint letting this shit fly,nigga get your ass out here! Souja stormed into Taye's bedroom,pulling Taye out of his room before he could even finish drying himself off or get himself dressed,Taye readjusting the towel around his naked waist as Souja pulled him out into open view.

Chill man! Taye spoke out to Souja,the dark flesh of Souja's strong hands gripping the light pale flesh of Taye's arms.Nigga i told you you was going get it,get on the fucking couch,you going get it in front of your moms,no more on the motherfucking down low,we going do this shit in the open,i dont give a fuck who watching nigga,nigga clearly you forgot who the top dog,the chief nigga! Souja yelled at Taye,still gripping tightly on

Taye's arms.Souja leave Taye alone,let that boy live his life,you not his man,and you not his father,it's a little girl in here! Latrelle pleaded to Souja,her eyes getting watery.Naw,i dont even wanna hear that right now man,Taye aint going nowhere,nigga going keep his ass here,and get what he got on the way! Souja spoke to Latrelle.

Souja pulled his hand under the couch next to him while continuing to hold onto Taye with his free hand,and then pulled a gun from under it,the gun surprising every face in the room.

Souja stop it,let Taye go,take me instead,let Taye and Kiana go,if you wanna do something to somebody do it to me,kill me,beat me,i dont care,just let my baby go! Latrelle shouted in tears to Souja,hoping she could take Taye's place,by sacrificing herself.Naw naw,sit the fuck back down,and take that little bitch over there with you,tell that little bitch to move her weave out the way so Taye can lay his ass down right there! Souja ordered Latrelle,wanting her to move Kiana and herself out of he and Taye's path.Souja didn't care about Latrelle's sacrificial offer,he just wanted Taye,Taye who he thought was a challenge,Taye who he lusted for since childhood,Taye who's innocence and youth he yearned for,Taye who he wanted to continue his rampage of sexual abuse on.

Little slut ass nigga,you always been my slut,nigga all you good for is a nut,Souja degraded Taye as Taye kept his head up,trying to keep some dignity,tho Souja's words and actions were getting to him.Get the fuck on the couch nigga,lay your ass down on your stomach,naw,as a matter of fact you going suck on the dick first,Souja commanded Taye,pushing Taye near the couch,while Latrelle and Kiana sat far at the corner of the room on the other couch,fear in their eyes.

Chapter 9

Is Taye going to be ok auntie? Kiana asked Latrelle silently,sensing that something wasn't quite right.Yea,he going be ok baby,we just gotta pray,Latrelle spoke calmly to

Kiana,not really sure of what was going to happen to Taye,not knowing if Taye was going to be raped or beaten,or both.Kiana baby go tell your mama imma do your hair tomorrow ok,im not feeling too good,Latrelle whispered to Kiana,wanting Kiana to leave the situation between Souja and Taye before it got even worse.Ok auntie Latrelle,Kiana spoke as she stood to her feet about to leave.Naw,let her see Taye get bitched,so she can follow his footsteps,then she would know how to take care of her man when she get a little older too,Souja smirked at Latrelle.

Souja you is fucking sick in your head right now,Latrelle spoke to Souja with disgust.Try me,tell that little bitch to leave again and watch me bust a cap in somebody,think im playing,Souja flashed his gun to Latrelle,Taye standing silently and nervously next to the couch.Man if you going do what you going do to me just do that shit somewhere else man,not in front of my mother man,and Kiana,thats some low ass shit Souja,this some foul and embarrassing shit man,Taye explained to Souja in deep emotion,hoping Souja could see reason.

Naw,was it foul when you was mouthing off at me in the bathroom earlier nigga,huh? Souja spoke to Taye.Man chill,this shit aint even worth it,Taye explained to Souja,trying to delay Souja's planned sexual assault.Im not saying i'll bust a cap in you,but nigga either you can get a bullet in you or some dick up in you,you pick nigga,which one? Souja spoke to Taye,Taye's eyes glistening a little,as if he wanted to cry.

Nigga dont even start that bitch ass crying,your moms then got the dick before,she know what it do,and that little girl over there probably too young to know whats going on,now nigga you the only one who need to get their shit together,Souja spoke to Taye angrily.Souja wanted to sexually abuse Taye in front of Latrelle and the little girl Kiana in hopes of somewhat breaking Taye's spirit and shaming him,but most of all to get his sick thrills from it,that was his primary goal.

Souja sat on the couch smoothly as he gapped his legs,and then gave Taye an inviting stare.Get down there nigga,Souja spoke to Taye as Taye got to his knees slowly in front of his crotch area,both he and Souja practically naked,wearing nothing but towels from their previous bathing processes.Souja gently moved Taye's head near his crotch as Taye trembled a little.Suck that dick nigga,Souja spoke silently to Taye as Taye's hand went underneath his towel,reaching for his manhood item.Taye began to take Souja's penis into his mouth as Souja moaned silently from the friction and warmth of it.

Ah,shit nigga,suck on that dick man! Souja moaned out to Taye in pleasure,Taye's head moving slowly up and down and around on Souja's stiffened penis.Why is his pee pee getting bigger like a sword auntie Latrelle? Kiana questioned Latrelle curiously,seeing Souja's hardened penis go in and out of Taye's mouth.Baby close your eyes,Latrelle ordered Kiana silently,not wanting her to see Taye's sexual abuse take place.Latrelle closed her own eyes as well,two teardrops falling from them as they shut.Latrelle couldn't bare to see Taye sexually assaulted right in front of her,tho she didn't consider herself the best mother in the world Taye was still her son,her baby,her child.

Naw Latrelle,open your eyes chick,Souja commanded Latrelle,wanting her to witness Taye's sexual abuse with her own eyes.Im not doing a motherfucking thing,this some nasty shit i wont be a part of,Latrelle spoke angrily to Souja.Taye i love you baby,it's going be over soon baby,i promise you that,Latrelle explained to Taye in emotion,her eyes still closed.

You closing your eyes and shit,i bet you aint got nothing to cover your ears,Souja spoke to Latrelle,and then pushing Taye's mouth harder and faster onto his erect penis,causing Taye to gag as his penis shoved nearly down his throat passage,Souja purposely wanting Latrelle to hear the gagging and slurping sounds of the forced oral sex he made Taye perform on him due to the fact that she couldn't see it,he at least wanted her to hear it.Tears began to roll down Latrelle's face heavily as she heard the sound of Souja's penis and Taye's mouth meeting.Souja enjoyed taking advantage of Taye,he liked having power over Taye,Taye's docile nature and innocence giving him thrills,regardless of Taye's male gender.

Souja laid himself back further onto the couch as he moaned deeply,continuing to violently shove Taye's head back and forth onto his penis,swiftly thrusting his crotch upward into Taye's full mouth.Get that shit wet,fuck! Souja moaned uncontrollably to Taye.Taye then spat onto Souja's penis,and quickly eased his open mouth down onto it,giving the shaft and tip a tease,and then devouring it again,letting it slither down near his throat,Taye wanting his unwanted situation with Souja to be over quickly.Oh shit little nigga! Souja moaned out loudly,a great deal pleasured by Taye's near swallowing of his penis.Stop man,stop stop,imma about to bust,Souja cautioned Taye quickly,feeling himself coming close to ejaculation.

Taye boldly kept his mouth glued to Souja's penis,secretly hoping Souja ejaculated,thinking that might end their vulgar situation sooner.Boy whats wrong with you,huh,you loving that dick huh,you want me to put that load in your mouth nigga,huh? Souja moaned and quivered to Taye as he gently stroked his big hands through Taye's short soft straight and damp hair strands.

Make love to that dick with your mouth nigga,Souja ordered Taye in pure ecstasy,Taye then dipping his mouth onto Souja's hard penis in a slow motion,letting his mouth circulate around Souja's throbbing penis as Souja's hand caressed the back of his head and face.Alright,thats enough man,i aint trying to bust yet nigga,i want some of this,i aint had this in a hot minute,Souja slid his hand down underneath Taye's towel,firmly grazing the smooth creases of Taye's bare buttocks.Taye removed his mouth from Souja's penis,and then stood to his feet again as Souja stood up from the couch as well,readjusting the towel around his waist as he stood towards the silent Taye.Souja stood close to Taye as their chests and towels and knees touched,and then began to passionately kiss Taye as if they were in love,Kiana opening her eyes slightly to witness it.

Auntie Latrelle are Taye and your boyfriend boyfriends too? Kiana questioned Latrelle silently.Baby just close your eyes,be quiet ok,Latrelle shushed Kiana.Yes maam,Kiana obeyed Latrelle,tho she continued to peep.Kiss me back nigga,Souja commanded Taye as Taye began to kiss him back with less passion.Get on the couch and get on your stomach,Souja ordered Taye,dropping his towel from his naked body to the hardwood floor,and then pulling Taye's towel off as Taye eased onto the couch,both he and Taye now in their full and complete nakedness.Ay latrelle! Souja called out to Latrelle calmly,Latrelle opening her eyes to an unpleasant view of Souja and Taye,Latrelle's eyes witnessing Souja's tall dark and muscled body hovering over and behind Taye's slender toned and slightly tall light body.Souja wet his right hand with his tongue,and then lubed himself with it,while making eye contact with Latrelle for just a second.

Damn,that ass nice and tight,better then pussy,Souja grunted in pleasure as he slowly glided himself inside of Taye before Latrelle's eyes,Taye flinching and gasping just a bit as Souja entered him.Look how he just took to that fat dick,that ass was made for me,since he was little,Souja spoke in his deep voice out loud,taunting Latrelle,and Taye.Sit your ass back down,Souja spoke to Latrelle as she stood to her feet moving Kiana away from her,Souja rubbing his gun sitting at the top of the couch with his free hand,while his other hand held onto his erect penis that was diving back and forth into Taye with strong strokes,Taye's face revealing the internal friction of it to Latrelle.

Take that dick like you used to dawg,you can handle it now nigga,you grown now! Souja yelled out to Taye as he continued to pound into his cavity from behind,Taye feeling Souja's penis travel through his inner fleshly tunnel.Taye began moaning out silently,unable to contain it,unable to not react to Souja's powerful strokes.The sound of Souja's naked flesh and testicles slapping against Taye's naked flesh echoed throughout the room,Latrelle covering Kiana's ears and then closing her own watery eyes again tightly.

Ah,ma im alright,this nigga aint breaking me! Taye lied in a vibrating voice,Souja now pounding him internally harder from behind,Souja's strong thighs gripping the sides of his own thighs.Souja then forced himself and Taye to fall to the edge of the couch as he folded one of Taye's legs

around his waist,slamming himself
mercilessly into Taye's body from the
side,while gripping Taye's neck,Taye's
vibrated moans filling the air,while
Souja pounded away for
more,enjoying the moans Taye
released from his lips.Latrelle
covered her own ears,nearly no
longer caring about covering Kiana's
ears,the trauma of Taye being
sexually assaulted piercing into her
like knives.

You trying get away from me and
now you still getting that pussy dug
out,just like when you was little,aint

nothing changed,im in your mind and body baby boy,but you aint never got it while we was naked,i should've been did it this way,shid,Souja gently bit and sucked on Taye's neck as Taye's head moved to the friction,Souja enjoying the naked exposed flesh of Taye's body,never really seeing Taye fully naked before,only with his underwear down.

Souja began to letup on Taye,slowing down his strokes inside of Taye,and then easing himself out of Taye smoothly,standing back to his feet as he masturbated himself slowly above Taye.Get on your back nigga,i aint done,now that you older i can really get up in you,get on your fucking back! Souja ordered Taye sternly.Taye laid himself on the couch,obeying Souja's order,his back to the cushions as Souja climbed on top of him.Souja then placed the tip of his penis near Taye's entrance,working it inside of Taye smoothly as Taye's mouth widened in a gasp.

Souja then began to push himself back and forth into Taye,causing Taye to moan out and whimper as the couch squeaked silently from their forced sexual friction.Nigga put your arms around me like you love me! Souja commanded Taye as he continued to sexually assault him on the couch.Taye hesitantly gripped Souja's moist and muscled back,feeling the strong structure of it,whimpers still escaping his lips.

Why are you hurting Taye?! Kiana spoke to Souja,opening her eyes again,hearing the pain in Taye's whimpers.Mind your motherfucking business! Souja yelled at Kiana while still thrusting himself into Taye,not caring if Kiana was watching.Baby come over here,Latrelle cried to Kiana as she pulled her into her arms.Nigga im murdering you with that dick boy! Souja boasted to Taye as he continued to plunge inside of him,now Pushing and grinding himself deeply into Taye's cavity,moving his hips around and around as if he and Taye were dancing to a rhythm,a forced rhythm,Souja's tight and round buttocks flexing.Jerk your dick nigga,oh you going like it too nigga,you going like it,and i should

bust in your mouth again,Souja spoke
to Taye.

You ready for that hot cum Taye?
Souja moaned silently to Taye.Tell me
nigga,say you want that hot cum,say
that shit out loud nigga,Souja ordered
Taye.I want your hot cum,Taye spoke
hesitantly and sadly to Souja,still
feeling Souja deep inside him.Souja
forcefully pushed himself into Taye
one last time with a deep grunt of
pleasure and then began to unload
his semen deep into Taye's
cavity,flooding Taye up with it,and
then pulling himself out of Taye to

shoot the rest of his ejaculating semen all over Taye's naked body.

Souja inhaled and exhaled in satisfaction after finishing his sexual assault on Taye,Taye still laying below him in anguish,soaked in his semen.Souja then used his penis to massage his warm thick and wet semen into Taye's nude semen covered flesh,rubbing it into Taye's exposed abs and crotch as if it were massaging oil.Why is that white stuff coming out of his pee pee auntie Latrelle,i thought only pee comes out,what is it? Kiana asked latrelle curiously,seeing nude Souja still slightly shooting and spilling himself over nude Taye.

Yea nigga,in front of your moms,and that little bitch,in front of them nigga,in front of them! Souja boasted to Taye,and then shoved his tongue deeply into Taye's mouth,french kissing Taye as Taye laid their nearly emotionless,while Latrelle eyed Souja's gun above the couch Taye had just been sexually abused on.

Chapter 10

Latrelle's eyes quickly focused off of Souja's gun as Souja reached for it slowly while still hovering his nude body over Taye's nude and wet body.Souja tightly pressed his fingers around the handle of the black steel gun,and then slowly slid the barrel of the gun along Taye's naked body,all the way up to Taye's mouth.Open your mouth nigga,Souja spoke silently to Taye as Taye slowly opened his mouth wider.Souja then placed the barrel of his gun inside of Taye's mouth,twirling it around and around the corners of Taye's mouth,Taye feeling the cool steel against the inside of his mouth,the rusty taste of the gun flavoring his mouth.

Nigga i should shoot your ass just for giving me a hard time,i aint never had to go through this when you was little,i just got the ass,you aint talk back or nothing,you just gave that pussy up,and took it like a soldier,you think you too grown now thats what it is,Souja explained to Taye as Taye listened to him with watery eyes.

Fuck you man,fuck you Souja,Taye spoke to Souja in a muffled voice,Souja's gun still inside his mouth.Oh fuck me huh,naw i fucked you little nigga,tore your little ass up,shit was good too,better than your mama,Souja antagonized Taye with a slight smirk.Souja then slipped his gun from Taye's mouth and then lurched himself up towards Taye's open mouth,his still slightly erect semen covered penis easing into Taye's mouth as his exposed crotch brushed against Taye's face.Taye could see Souja's strands of pubic hairs and hard abs in full view of his face as Souja pressed himself farther down into his mouth.

Souja began moving himself up and down inside of Taye's mouth as if he was making love to Taye's mouth,his penis gagging Taye as it slid down his throat,showing an imprint of it's huge size on the outside of Taye's jaws.Taste that cum nigga,Souja swirled his penis around in Taye's mouth and then slowly pulling it out to slap Taye along the face with it.You done man,let me roll out man,Taye spoke to Souja,Souja now beating Taye's naked chest with his heavy penis as he bit his lip in lust.Im done when i say im done little fucker,Souja spoke back to Taye,his eyes locking on Taye's face.Souja positioned his naked genitals slightly above Taye's exposed knee,and then began to dry the wetness from his penis with his towel that laid on the floor next to the couch he and Taye forcefully shared inappropriately while Latrelle and Kiana witnessed.

Taye studied Souja's posture carefully,and then quickly kneed Souja in the groins,causing Souja to squeal out in pain as he fell to the far edge of the couch holding his genitals. Taye quickly got to his feet and then ran towards the telephone, hoping to call for help. Imma kill you little nigga, touch that phone and watch me end your ass! Souja grunted in pain to Taye while aiming his gun at him, standing to his feet while still holding his hand inbetween his legs, his genitals still kind of sore from Taye's swift knee action.

Nigga you think you did something, nigga just for that imma fuck your bitch ass again, Souja explained to Taye,Taye freezing in place,his hand almost reaching the telephone that sat only a few inches away from his fingertips.Souja gathered himself together,finally feeling the pain of his genitals fade as he headed over to Taye.You want the dick again,huh,thats what you want little nigga,Souja whispered into Taye's ear as he forced his nude body behind Taye's nude body,agressively kissing Taye all over his neck and cheek,Taye powerless to do anything.

Taye yanked himself slightly away from Souja,but not enough to break away from his grip.You trying be tough nigga,you going give me some of that pussy again,Souja spoke to Taye silently,his hands rubbing up and down Taye's body as annoyance and sadness covered Taye's face.Hurry up baby,go! Latrelle quickly ordered Kiana out of the house,wanting her to get away from all the commotion.

Ay man that little girl going go run her motherfucking mouth! Souja yelled at Latrelle,angry at her letting Kiana escape out the front door,feeling Kiana might tell about he and Taye's forced encounter.Souja leave that little girl alone,she probably dont even know what the fuck was going on in here,you is a dirty grimy ass motherfucker! Latrelle explained to Souja.Latrelle you stunting like that huh,i got you,get your ass over there on the couch,and here,bring your gay cum disposing ass son with you,Souja pushed Taye into Latrelle,forcing both of them towards the couch.

Baby im sorry,im so sorry,i understand if you hate me for the rest of your life,i fucking deserve it baby,Latrelle cradled Taye in her arms as if he were a baby,tho he still was her baby.Im cool ma,im alright,Taye lied to Latrelle with a pained facial expression.Taye Reached for his towel that rested on the floor,drying himself with it,and then gently pulling it back around his naked waist,partially covering his nakedness,while Souja still stood in his full nudity in front of him and Latrelle.Shid,if that little broad snitch imma go down like a real nigga,fuck all that,imma have me some fun with yall two,mother and son,two whores,a female whore and a gay ass whore that came out of her,Souja snickered.

Take this off Latrelle,Souja pointed his gun to Latrelle's blouse.Souja just leave,all this shit is uncalled for! Latrelle shouted to Souja.Take all your shit off,i aint playing right now,do what the fuck i said,Souja commanded Latrelle smoothly.Taye help your moms take off her shit,Souja ordered Taye.Naw man,this is fucking wrong dawg,all this shit! Taye explained to Souja in tears.

Latrelle began to undress herself,taking off her blouse first,and then unfastening her bra,then removing her pants and panties,joining Taye and Souja in their nakedness,Taye still sitting silently beside her while Souja still stood above them both.Aint that a nice sight,a mama and her baby,let me give yall a little shower,Souja spoke to Latrelle and Taye as he began to masturbate himself above them,slapping his penis across both their faces.

Come here little nigga,aint nobody tell you to put a towel back around your waist,take that shit off,Souja threw Taye's towel from his naked body,placing Taye's mouth onto his penis,while groping Latrelle's exposed breasts.Pussy ass nigga,bitching you and your moms at the same time,you aint about that life like me little dude,imma thorough nigga,Souja spoke to Taye,while still interacting sexually with both Taye and Latrelle,moans escaping his lips as Taye continued to perform his forced oral sex on him.

Alright,go get your ass dressed Latrelle,you about to watch Taye get bitched again,little Taye aint learn from the last time,Souja spoke to Latrelle.Latrelle placed her clothes back on as she got to her feet again,Souja still placing Taye's mouth up and down on his penis.You about to get a facial nigga,Souja spoke to Taye as he stood to his feet,hovering above Taye.Souja masturbated himself over Taye,but stopped his hand friction once he and Taye and Latrelle heard three taps at the front door.Latrelle go see who it is,and dont say shit,Souja ordered Latrelle to the front door.Nigga and you better keep your ass quiet,Souja then commanded Taye.

Who is it? Latrelle answered the front door in a strained voice.It's Earl,do Taye live here? the man outside the door spoke to Latrelle.He gone right now,Latrelle lied to Earl.Wait,Latrelle is that you? Earl spoke to Latrelle,waiting for her to answer.Oh,yea,this me Earl,how you been? Latrelle stuttered to Earl nervously.I been cool,I saw Taye at school,i work there at the college,saw Taye name while i was grading papers,i almost lost my damn mind,i got yall address from student files,i had to see Taye again,Earl explained to Latrelle through the door.We alright now,i hope the bad blood between us is gone and shit,we cool? Earl spoke to Latrelle,his voice anxious.Look,Earl,come back another time,i tell Taye you came through,Latrelle explained to Earl.Damn,can i at least see your face Latrelle,i aint seen you and Taye in years,whats good,how you been? Earl spoke to Latrelle.

Latrelle turned around slowly to Souja,wanting his permission to open the door.Let that nigga in,Souja spoke to Latrelle as he began to get himself dressed again,but forcing Taye to stay naked.Latrelle slowly opened the front door,now staring Earl directly in the eyes,remembering him just as before,seeing his face for the first time in years.Girl you still look the same,Earl spoke to latrelle with a smile.I know,it's been awhile,i been doing good,you still look the same too,Latrelle spoke back to Earl,trying to keep her nerves under control.But just tell Taye i see him at school,imma about to leave,nice seeing you,Earl turned to leave from the doorway,but being grabbed by Latrelle before he could fully leave the doorway.Earl call the police,leave,Souja got a gun,he then raped Taye! Latrelle quickly informed Earl,disobeying Souja.Get your ass in here,Souja snatched Latrelle from the doorway quickly,and then placing Earl at gunpoint.

Naw,get in here man,Souja spoke silently to Earl,guiding him inside by the barrel of his gun.Earl then quickly turned himself towards Souja to wrestle with him,Earl trying desperately to get the gun from Souja's strong grip,the door slamming behind them as they fell to the living area floor still in a wrestling match,tho Souja started to gain the upperhand.Old faggot ass nigga! Souja shouted out to Earl as he flipped Earl on his back with force.Old bitch ass nigga! Souja began to violently kick Earl in his side,causing Earl to gasp in pain,Earl holding his ribcage.Latrelle jumped onto Souja's back,trying to assist Earl in wrestling Souja down,tho she had no real affect.

Souja swung Latrelle from his back,and then continued to stomp Earl,kicking Earl in his face and side.Watch your little uncle get his ass beat nigga! Souja explained to Taye,while pointing his gun at Taye.Earl then suddenly and finally managed to bring Souja down while Souja boasted about his win,Earl gripping his arms around Souja's leg,causing Souja to trip and fall to the hardwood floor.

You the bitch ass nigga! Earl began to pummel Souja as he got on top of him.You aint doing nothing you faggot ass nigga! Souja yelled to Earl,trying to regain the upperhand on Earl again.Souja gave Earl a swift punch in the jaw,but Earl kept swinging away at him,giving him strong blows to the face,Souja gasping in pain,and then protecting his face with his arms.

Imma about to kill you nigga! Souja shouted out to Earl,cocking his gun,and then trying to place it towards Earl's face as Earl restrained his hands with all his might.Taye quickly rushed over to Earl's aid,grabbing ahold of the gun along with Earl and Souja,both he and Earl trying to get the gun away from Souja's hand.Earl punched Souja one more time with his free hand,causing Souja to slightly lose grip of the gun,Taye now prying each one of Souja's fingers away from the gun one by one,until the gun fired off,the gun falling to the floor in a clapping sound from Souja's fingers.Taye and Earl checked themselves for bullet wounds,but neither of them were shot,and neither was Souja.

Taye and Earl then turned their heads towards Latrelle,hearing her heavy breathing,and then examining the bullet wound in her chest,a wound that was bleeding badly.Souja's gun had accidently fired off at Latrelle,but was initially meant for Earl.

Ma! Taye quickly ran over to Latrelle,applying pressure to her wound,in hopes of stopping the bleeding.Get the fuck off me nigga! Souja violently and quickly shoved Earl off of him,quickly running out of the front door away from Earl,Taye,and the badly wounded Latrelle,knowing that police would be involved soon,and that he would be in trouble with the law.Souja quickly fled the area and neighborhood,not caring about taking any of his belongings with him,his car zooming down the street as his tires screeched.

Earl headed over to Taye and Latrelle,his lip busted from his fight with Souja.You going be alright ma,Taye explained to Latrelle while still holding her wound,Latrelle's

warm blood staining her blouse.Taye
quickly headed over to the telephone
and then called for an
ambulance.Taye then headed back
over to Latrelle,wanting to assist
her.Man Souja going get his,your
mother told me he raped you and
now that i think about it that was him
who was molesting you way back
when you was a little something,they
took me away from you and now let's
pray Souja aint take your mama away
from you,Earl explained to Taye in a
apologetic low tone of voice,gloom
on his face.

Go get yourself dressed Taye,i know you cold,i'll look after your mama,Earl spoke softly to Taye,Taye heading into his bedroom for fresh clothing to put on,but instead breaking down into huge tears,his light face flushed with the color red.Taye had lost so much at the hands of Souja,his innocence,his pride,and maybe his own mother.

Ambulance sirens soon echoed outside of the house where Taye and his uncle Earl,and his slowly dying mother Latrelle waited,the ambulance sirens followed by police sirens as well.

Chapter 11

Tho Taye was mentally scarred on the inside he continued to live his life,allowing himself to find happiness,despite of what he felt on the inside,tho it was very hard at times.

Souja had gotten away,but police continued their search for him,and later on finding his body gunned down to death in an alleyway after being robbed and then killed for silence,forensics stating Souja died a painful and slow death from his bullet wounds while choking on his own blood.

The vile acts of Souja were mentally burned into Taye's head forever,tho Taye moved forward from his horrors at the hands of Souja day by day,with the assistance of his uncle Earl,and a few loving words from Latrelle before she died in the hospital of her gunshot wound.

The end

(Note to readers)

This book is in no way a reflection on the authors personal views of sexual abuse and violence or glorifying it or condoning it,but simply shining light on the touchy subject in his own way.

This book was meant to enlighten whom it may on subjects of pedophilia and homosexuality,and violence.

The book was meant to show that perpetrators sometimes go unnoticed in clear view while the stereotypes society has placed to the forefront regarding homosexuality and other groups of minorities gets noticed without fair trial or fair judgement,and are more than often believed and judged incorrectly due to the mistakes of a handful in that one group based on stereotyping,fear,and hate.